LONDON TRANSPORT BUSES
in Colour 1955-1969

Ian Allan

60th

ANNIVERSARY

Kevin McCormack

Diesel Domination

Front cover: This view at Waltham Cross was taken between 25 April 1959, when trolleybus route 659 was replaced by RM-operated route 259, and 18 July 1959, when route 649 succumbed to the ever-mighty motor bus. Class K3 No 1678 dating from 1940 stands beside new RM661 at the old terminus. *Marcus Eavis*

North/South Divide

Back cover: The creation of Crawley New Town and the development of nearby Gatwick Airport brought a need for more integrated bus services linking the industrial areas to the north of the town (in LT's territory) with the new residential areas to the south (served by Southdown). In January 1958, LT's local 483 service was replaced by Southdown's route 23 from Brighton and a new route 23A. This summer 1965 scene at Crawley bus station depicts RT3205 alongside Southdown's finest. *Marcus Eavis*

Spoilt for Choice

Title page: Three routes are on offer at Edgware station on this summer Sunday in 1968. The smart trio are, from left to right, RTs 3740, 2528 and 3474. *Marcus Eavis*

Wrong Bus

Right: Whatever Shakespeare's association with Victoria, he would have been ill advised to return to Stratford on RTL416! This summer 1967 view features two of this declining class which LT grew to dislike, withdrawing the final Leyland versions 11 years earlier than the last RTs. *Roy Hobbs*

Escaped Tigers

Far right: Limited garage capacity at Kingston forced buses to park out on the road on Sundays, when there were fewer services. TD82 heads a line of eight Leyland Tigers in Wood Street in 1959. *Marcus Eavis*

First published 2002

ISBN 0 7110 2881 8

Published by Ian Allan Publishing

an imprint of Ian Allan Publishing Ltd, Hersham, Surrey KT12 4RG.
Printed by Ian Allan Printing Ltd, Hersham, Surrey KT12 4RG.

Code:0203/B2

Introduction

I am pleased to present a further historic colour album on London Transport ('LT') buses and trolleybuses.

These albums are, of course, only possible through the continuing supply of largely unpublished, good-quality photographs (slides), and it is particularly rewarding this time to be able to feature so many scenes from the 1950s, when few photographers were working in colour.

Many of the buses featured in this volume lasted through to the 1970s and are seen here in their prime: well turned out and often freshly painted. The absence in the earlier shots of trafficator 'ears', fitted throughout the fleet in 1959/60, is an added bonus. On the other hand, there are some classes of bus and trolleybus featured which never made it into the 1960s. And, of course, *all* the trolleybuses had left London's streets by May 1962.

I make no apologies for the fact that the vehicles featured in this book reflect my own preference for the types I associate with my childhood, including Routemasters. My very first Ian Allan spotting book (the early-1955 edition) featured a drawing of a Routemaster on the cover. I have made a concession to modernity by including photographs of XAs, XFs and FRM1, but RC and Merlin enthusiasts will be disappointed. On the other hand, admirers of London's prewar vehicles, seldom photographed in colour while in service, are in for a treat. Since settling on the period 1955-69 for the title of the book, I have obtained some images from the early 1950s which, thanks to technological advances, have reproduced better than expected, and I am delighted to have been able to include these as late entries.

I should like to thank the photograph contributors for allowing me to use their precious material: Marcus Eavis, Dave Brown, the late Mike Harries, Roy Hobbs, John Aldridge, Bruce Jenkins, Geoff Rixon, John Webb, Maurice Bateman and John Bishop. Photographs by Jack Wyse and from the Frank Hunt Collection are held by the Light Rail Transit Association, London Area. Thanks are also due to Judith Barnes for exploring Hertfordshire and Essex with me, to Jim Joyce for his contacts and to John Aldridge (again) for the loan of maps etc. Finally, I am grateful to Tony Beard for arranging to have the colour photograph on page 47 revitalised, as this had faded badly.

The caption information was derived mainly from the following books published by Capital Transport: *RT — The Story of a London Bus* by Ken Blacker (1979), *London Trolleybus Routes* by Hugh Taylor (1994), *London Buses in the 1950s* by Ken Glazier (1989) and *London Buses in the 1960s*, also by Ken Glazier (1998).

I hope the images in this book will bring back happy memories to older readers and provide an interesting perspective on London's bygone public road transport (Routemasters excepted!) for historians and those too young to have been there at the time.

Kevin R. McCormack
Ashtead, Surrey
November 2001

3

Downhill Struggle

Above: The short-wheelbase 'B1'-class trolleybus dating from 1935 had a special braking system to enable these vehicles to descend Anerley Hill's 1-in-9 gradient safely. In 1958, No 85 gingerly makes its way down from Crystal Palace. *Marcus Eavis*

All Aboard

Right: Farningham's main street is deserted but RT4723 is well filled as it passes through this Kent village on its way to the south eastern suburbs in the summer of 1969. Two years later, one-person-operated AEC Swift single-deckers replaced the RTs. *Dave Brown*

Shanty Town

Below: In the 1950s Heathrow Airport was owned and managed by the Government, with modernisation being a slow process. Here, in July 1955, we see TD86 standing beside LT-operated BEA 1½-deck airport coach NLP 641. A Ministry-owned Austin Devon van (with windows) is parked behind. *Jack Wyse*

Sea Change

Right: Intended for the warmer climes of South Africa, 43 British-built trolleybuses ended up instead in Ilford, East London, largely due to wartime shipping risks. Being non-standard in so many respects, these vehicles inevitably became early candidates for replacement by buses, running for the last time on 18 August 1959. No 1751, originally destined for Johannesburg, leaves the Chadwell Heath terminus of route 693 shortly before withdrawal. *Marcus Eavis*

Mystery Tour

Above and right: RT3012 approaches Cockshot Hill, Reigate, in June 1969, carrying passengers seemingly going nowhere, only to return shortly after. Perhaps this was a short working of route 424 — we shall never know for certain. The now-demolished former East Surrey offices and garage in Bell Street, on the corner of Lesbourne Road, are clearly evident in the background. *Mike Harries*

Going round in Circles

Left: Trolleybus route 602 provided an anti-clockwise service around the Kingston Loop starting and ending at the Dittons, where this view was taken five days before the end of trolleybus operation in London (8 May 1962). Route 603 operated from Tolworth in the opposite direction.
Geoff Rixon

A Moment in Time

Below: This is Clarence Street, Kingston, on a typical working day in the spring of 1962, as seen from an approaching trolleybus: a conductor without his bus, a wonderful array of what would now be classic cars, and trolleybus No 1386 heading off to Wimbledon — a slice of history!
Marcus Eavis

On Death Row

Above: Several forward-entrance, Country Area STLs ended up here at Cohen's Penhall Road scrapyard, Charlton, in November 1951, alongside redundant trams. Five of these STLs secured a life extension of 10 years, through being converted to tree-loppers (one of which survives today), but the vehicle in the foreground, STL960, was not so lucky. *Jack Wyse*

Slide Rule

Right: The provincial design features of the RLH class are epitomised by the absence of wind-down side windows in this May 1967 view of RLH70 passing Spiers' delightful coal office at Kenton. *Geoff Rixon*

13

Airport Stop-over

Left: Looking resplendent is low-height RLH28 on a visit to the 1964 Biggin Hill Air Fair in Kent. This was the last year of RLH operation on route 410. *Marcus Eavis*

Class Distinction

Above: A contrast in road transport is provided by an Austin Princess Limousine and AEC Regal, T744, at Uxbridge in 1957. These Weymann-bodied buses, with seating capacity for 32 passengers, were introduced in 1946. *Marcus Eavis*

Levelled Crossing

Below and right: Forty years on, there is no sign of Raynes Crossing, the signalbox and cottage having long been demolished. These early-1962 shots depict trolleybuses 1477 and 1518 heading north along West Barnes Lane, between Motspur Park and Raynes Park. Route 604 was replaced by an extension of the 131 bus service. *Marcus Eavis*

Two's Company

Above: XF8 is the outsider here among the red Routemasters at Finsbury Square. The XFs — eight Daimler Fleetlines with Park Royal bodies — were the first new-generation buses for LT and were normally based at East Grinstead. When this picture was taken, in April 1966, they had just been exchanged with eight Leyland Atlanteans for comparative trials. *Marcus Eavis*

Smoking Compartment

Right: From its entry into service on 26 June 1967, the one and only front-entrance, rear-engined Routemaster, FRM1, lacked opening windows until the Fire Brigade produced a hammer on 31 August 1967! The vehicle was fortunate to survive an engine fire, and when it re-entered service in December 1967 it sported nine opening windows. Before the fire, FRM1 was photographed from the footbridge joining Waterloo station to the Shell Centre, proceeding along York Road.
Marcus Eavis

Shady Nook

Above: Saunders-bodied RT1870 nestles under a large tree in Placehouse Lane, Old Coulsdon, in the summer of 1964. The Tudor-style buildings and concrete posts remain today and in place of the RT there will still be a red double-decker — probably an Alexander-bodied Dennis Trident on route 60. *John Aldridge*

Blind Turning

Right: This Green Line coach, modernised RF205, is heading for Dorking garage, but the driver has anticipated its return to Dunstable by changing the destination indicator early. It's summer 1968, and the retailers of this charming market town are also into blinds — a wonderful array rarely seen nowadays. The shopping bags at the stop are waiting patiently for a bus. *Mike Harries*

No Chance

Above: If this crowd at Welling Corner in November 1951 is hoping to board Q140 then most are probably in for a disappointment, because the 1936-built AEC looks pretty full already. Sidcup garage's route 241 was the last Central Area service on which Qs operated, replacements eventually appearing in the form of new RFs in March 1953. *Jack Wyse*

Clapham Omnibus

Below: This vehicle, seen passing the well-known common in March 1951, was 'for all' — providing they could afford Green Line coach fares! TF81 belonged to the 88-strong class of Leyland Tigers built to a revolutionary design and perpetuating the side-mounted-engine concept of the earlier Q type. On the right stands an Austin Seven box saloon identical to one owned by the author and which was parked quite recently at virtually the same spot while research was carried out for another title. *Jack Wyse*

New age traveller

Left and above: Guildford Woman alights from RF599 in June 1969, probably unaware that this modern-looking vehicle left the drawing-board nearly 20 years earlier. The dramatic contrast with 1948-built TD32, photographed at Kingston, illustrates the generation gap created over just a couple of years. Was the RF simply ahead of its time or the TD plain antiquated? *Dave Brown/John Webb*

Ant's-eye View

Above: The camera angle seems to accentuate the old-fashioned, STL-like appearance of low-height double-decker RLH69. This mid-1960s view was taken in Front Lane, Cranham, directly opposite the gates of Upminster Underground depot. 'Bon Bon' in Moor Lane has now become a travel agent and the tubular bus shelter has given way to a newer structure, but route 248 still terminates here, operated by FirstGroup. *Maurice Bateman*

Sense of Belonging

Above: LT has attached its imprint firmly onto Windsor garage, but within months all references to LT would be eradicated, upon transfer of its Country Bus & Coach Department to London Country on 1 January 1970.

This 1969 shot depicts two Green Line coaches — lengthened Routemaster RCL2234 and modernised Regal IV RF252 — preparing to set off on their long journeys to the other side of London. *Marcus Eavis*

Double Header

Below: Two heads appear in the cab of RTW103, creating the impression that the driver is sitting in the instructor's lap, as this Hendon-based trainer passes through Hampton Court in the autumn of 1966. The 500 members of this class of Leylands had all been withdrawn by 15 May 1966, but, being 8ft wide instead of 7ft 6in (the normal width of the RT family), they were eminently suitable for use as driver-training buses, being the same width as Routemasters. *Geoff Rixon*

Stay of Execution

Below: The decision to sell the postwar 'Q1' trolleybuses to Spain meant that the last two trolleybus depots, Fulwell and Isleworth, had to be re-equipped with surplus older types. This view at Finchley depot dates from just before buses took over on 8 November 1961, whereupon the 'L3' trolleybuses in the picture migrated to Fulwell for a final six months of service. *Marcus Eavis*

Short-time Working

Left and below left: On 30 September 1951 LT took over local services in the Grays/Tilbury area from Eastern National but had insufficient buses to run them. Consequently 28 vehicles were made available to LT for three months by the area's former operator, although not all were needed. LT took over the Eastern National garage at Argent Street, Grays, but intended to close it and decided not to have new garage stencil-plates made. Instead, GY plates were used, painted orange to distinguish the allocation from vehicles based at LT's existing Hogg Lane garage. These two exceptionally rare colour images depict Eastern National 3897, a 1946 Bristol L5G, on route 85 (later covered by RT-operated routes 328 and 328A) and 3721, a Bristol JO5G dating from 1937. The LT bus stops are new. *Jack Wyse*

Tricky Situation

Right: LT was in a different sort of pickle during the latter part of 1950, when it was trying to find a use for the redundant Green Line Daimler CWA6s displaced at Romford by new RTs. A lack of decision-making caused the Daimlers to be delicensed before Merton garage saved the day by agreeing to take the lot. Green Line fleetnames were removed, and repainting into red livery followed over several months. This scene, at the largely unaltered top of Whitehall (east side), dates from April 1951 and depicts what is believed to be D153, still wearing its two-tone green livery. *Jack Wyse*

Winning Formula

Below right: The ultra-reliable RT was a safe bet for taking spectators from London to the motor-racing circuit at Brands Hatch in Kent — a task which could not necessarily be safely entrusted to more modern types. Playing the role of the luxury coach is RT4723, photographed at Victoria in 1969. *Dave Brown*

Going to the Dogs

Above: When the ever-growing fleet of Routemasters had seen off the last trolleybuses, the RT family of buses was next in line. Some sales of standard postwar vehicles had occurred as early as January 1958, due to over-ordering and service reductions, but, once replacement started in earnest, LT decided to eliminate the Leylands first because they were unpopular with drivers and engineering staff. Here we see Wimbledon Coaches' former RTL746 taking punters to the local greyhound stadium in 1967. *Marcus Eavis*

Tootling through Tooting

Above: This 1960 shot shows trolleybus No 1076 in Mitcham Road, about to pass Tooting Broadway station. The location is comparatively unchanged today, except that the shop on the left is now just plain 'Woolworths' and is dwarfed by a new Marks & Spencer building next door. *Marcus Eavis*

Reds to the Rescue

Above: A shortage of serviceable green RFs caused the Country Area to borrow some red examples in 1967 (and at other times as well). This view down Prices Lane (to the south of Reigate) shows a resplendent RF387 standing at the point where the road becomes Sandcross Lane. Gone today, of course, are the Morris Oxford and Austin Cambridge cars and also the bus shelter, but just about everything else is still extant. Even route 430 survives, but with blue and yellow buses operated by Metrobus. *Roy Hobbs*

Race to the Races

Right: In June 1967 Derby Day (in those days a Wednesday) was blessed with fine weather, and the express bus service linking the most southerly Underground station with Epsom Downs did a roaring trade. Recently repainted RT4227 from Thornton Heath garage has just dropped off the 'punters' at Tattenham Corner, where the horses turn into the final straight. *Roy Hobbs*

Return of the Roundel

Above: A few months before the roof-mounted LT logo made way for the London Country emblem (from 1 January 1970), RFs 539 and 621 and an unidentified RT stand at Leatherhead garage. Surprisingly, the roundel-based 'Enquiries' sign survived right up until the garage's demolition in May 1999. Then, lo and behold, in August 2001, LT bus stops incorporating the famous roundel reappeared at this spot. *Marcus Eavis*

Dismal Docklands

Right: Today's prestigious development on the Isle of Dogs is far removed from this early-1959 scene at the West India Docks terminus of the 677 service to Smithfield Market. Trolleybuses ran here for the last time on 14 April 1959. Note the old-style 'deep' bus-stop flag. *Marcus Eavis*

Deer Stalker

Left: Merton garage's RT469 crosses Bushy Park, near Hampton Court, in the autumn of 1962 on its way from Feltham to Mitcham. Working of route 152 by RTs ceased upon its conversion to one-person Merlin operation on 24 January 1970. *Marcus Eavis*

Loss Leader

Below: Leyland trolleybus No 1261 from 1939, with another in its wake, passes through Whipps Cross on its way from Woodford to Bloomsbury — the nearest trolleybuses got to London's West End. Route 581 was particularly uneconomic, with poor passenger loadings outside peak hours, and withdrawal was brought forward to 14 April 1959. *Marcus Eavis*

Taking Turns

Left: The Highgate Village turning-circle was created in 1939 when trolleybus route 611 to Moorgate was introduced. Class J3 No 1048 from Holloway depot was photographed shortly before the service was replaced by the 271 bus route on 20 July 1960. *Marcus Eavis*

Above: Six years later, the village is host to Leyland Atlantean XA12 and Daimler Fleetline XF7 during their comparative trials. *Marcus Eavis*

Country Roads

Below right: Having set out from St Albans, RT3442 heads along the B158 near Essendon, Hatfield, at its junction with Bedwell Avenue and the lane to Letty Green in the winter of 1968/9. A learner driving a Morris Minor is in pursuit. The landscape and trees remain unchanged today. *Dave Brown*

High Profile

Right: Class L3 trolleybus No 1521 had a busy day on 8 May 1962, working the commemorative run with No 1 in the afternoon and then being decorated for the final run into Fulwell depot that night. Through the generosity of Cohen's, the scrap merchant, No 1521 was saved for posterity. *Marcus Eavis*

Commemorating London's Trolleybuses 1931 to 1962 ⊖

LONDON'S
LAST
TROLLEYBUSES
8 May 1962

1521

LONDON TRANSPORT

Trials and Tribulations

Above: In its four-year life with LT which began in October 1962, the pioneer forward-entrance Routemaster, RMF1254, was demonstrated to Liverpool, East Kent and Halifax, but failed to attract orders. In between time, the bus was either out of service or, as seen here at Heathrow in May 1965, on loan to British European Airways. Eventually, some stability entered its life when it was sold to Northern General, the only non-London operator to buy new Routemasters, which, as it happens, were of the same design as RMF1254. *Marcus Eavis*

Old School

Right: One-person operation (OPO) in the Central Area, which had been phased out in 1949, was reintroduced in 1964, and, as the new generation of buses such as the Merlins and Swifts had not yet emerged, RFs were used. RF421 is seen passing the famous Harrow School in August 1969, working route 136. This was a new OPO service introduced on 8 August 1966 to link Harrow-on-the-Hill and South Harrow stations via Harrow Village. *Marcus Eavis*

Passing Shot

Left: A little bit of luck provides the photographer with two for the price of one as 'J3' No 1053 and 'L1' No 1362 meet on Highgate Hill, shortly before cessation on 19 July 1960. Only trolleybuses fitted with special braking equipment were allowed on this 1-in-10 gradient, unfitted trolleybuses having to terminate at Archway station. *Marcus Eavis*

Roaming Regent

Below left: Given that there were only 76 members of the RLH class and the majority were painted green, it was not too uncommon for Country Area ones to be drafted into the Central Area when a red one was off the road. A case in point was the loan, in summer 1961, of RLH11 to Harrow Weald garage for the 230 service. This view of the vehicle is at Rayners Lane. *Marcus Eavis*

Soldiering On

Above: Pride of the Green Line coach fleet just before and immediately after World War 2 were the 10T10s, comprising 266 vehicles. T647, photographed at the now-demolished Staines garage, was one of the class which lasted long enough to work the Southern orbital route from Gravesend to Windsor, which started on 1 July 1953. During the war, the 10T10s served with the US Forces or as ambulances. *John Aldridge*

Sheltered Spot

Left: The pleasant village of South Mimms, surprisingly close to the roaring M25 and nearby Service Area, has escaped the march of 'progress'. After some 34 years, virtually everything in this picture remains today apart from the bin and the bus stop in the foreground, the flag having subsequently been attached to the lamp-post. Naturally, RT3784 has departed for good, but route 298, now operated by ARRIVA, still serves this bus shelter. *Dave Brown*

Boarding Party

Above: Fulwell's trolleybus No 1395 is a popular choice for these passengers waiting to cross the Thames at Kingston in early 1962. The Bentalls backdrop is still *in situ* today. *Marcus Eavis*

Escaping the Crowds

Above: Onslow Street bus station in Guildford seems to be guarded by a prison officer in this busy scene depicting RLH46 heading off towards the low bridge in Chertsey Lane, Staines. *Dave Brown*

Doubtful Pedigree

Above: Red Rover of Aylesbury was one of several operators to take advantage of LT's decision to rid itself of the Cravens RTs after only seven years of service. Former RT1482, with its roof-box removed, stands at this northwestern LT outpost in 1961, in company with two City of Oxford AEC Regents and a United Counties Bristol LD. *Marcus Eavis*

Electric Shock

Above: When trolleybus route 654, which had replaced the preceding tram route in December 1935, was itself supplanted by motor buses in March 1959, no-one would have believed that, some 40 years later, electric traction in the form of trams would once again pass this spot. Class B1 No 93 picks up in Tamworth Road, West Croydon, in 1955. *Bruce Jenkins*

Flying Start

Right: One of the first duties of these brand-new Routemasters, which entered service in May 1966, was to operate the shuttle service from Bromley North station to the Biggin Hill International Air Fair where this view was taken. RMLs 2446 and 2459 belonged to the final batch of green Routemasters, which in fact became the last new double-deckers allocated by LT to the Country Area before the takeover by London Country Bus Services on 1 January 1970. *Marcus Eavis*

Fit for a King

Above: Two of London's finest trolleybuses, members of the postwar 'Q1' class, stand outside Hampton Court Palace in the summer of 1957. The extra 6in in width which these vehicles provided would no doubt have been welcomed by King Henry VIII! Four years after this photograph was taken, the 'Q1s' were operating in Spain. *Jack Wyse*

Look Smart

Right: A daytime journey from Kent to Buckinghamshire via Central London was never going to be fast, but the restyling and refitting of 175 Green Line RFs in the mid-1960s helped create an illusion of modernity and speed. RF62 brightens up the southern end of the Edgware Road near Maida Vale in May 1967. *Geoff Rixon*

Over the Hill

Above: There are only a few weeks to go before the abandonment of what was once the largest trolleybus network in the world. Class L3

No 1512 descends Cambridge Road, Kingston, on a short working of route 605 from Teddington in early 1962. *Marcus Eavis*

Bus Block

Above: At Dorking in the spring of 1969, RT3202 encounters the age-old problem of being unable to pull up at the bus stop due to a parked vehicle. Route 414 was largely converted to Routemaster operation on 1 January 1972, following the displacement of the Green Line Routemaster coaches from Romford and Grays. *Dave Brown*

Out of Place

Above: Five trolleybus routes purported to terminate at Moorgate, in the City of London's 'square mile', but in fact they reached no further than Finsbury Square, which was outside the City boundary. At least three of these routes are represented in this 1960 view outside Finsbury Square House.

Right: Route 639 was withdrawn on 31 January 1961. Five years later, Leyland Atlantean XA18 takes No 1552's place, at Hampstead Heath. *Marcus Eavis*

Still Standing

Above: Redundant garages seldom survive, but the trolleybus shed and entrance offices at Carshalton (actually located in Westmead Road, Sutton) have cheated demolition and remain in commercial use today. Opened in 1906 as a tram depot, the building became a trolleybus depot in 1935 and a bus garage when route 654 was withdrawn on 3 March 1959, eventually closing on 28/29 January 1964. *Marcus Eavis*

Speeding Springbok

Right: This action shot, in which everything seems to be moving (!), was taken in Ilford High Road at the junction with Hainault Street. The trolleybus is Class SA2 No 1743, which was intended for (but never reached) Durban in South Africa. Notice the darkened windows and permanently locked sliding exit door. *Frank Hunt collection*

61

Off to the Flicks

Left: You can forget the West End hotel, theatre and cabbages; this Savoy was a cinema in Teddington and the terminus of trolleybus route 605. Here we see 'Q1' No 1817 in all its magnificence outside Wimbledon Town Hall in 1957. *Marcus Eavis*

Rail-Air Link

Right: In 1958, when this picture was taken, the author (accompanied by his long-suffering mother) went on a plane-spotting expedition from Ealing to Stapleford Tawney Aerodrome. We travelled by Central Line Underground to Theydon Bois and thence by TD-operated route 250 to the location shown here outside the aircraft hangars (behind the photographer). Apart from the absence of TD87, this scene is virtually unchanged today. *Marcus Eavis*

64

Advancing Enemy

Left and above: Trolleybus services 629 and 641 shared much of the same route and were due for simultaneous withdrawal. In the event, the 629 was replaced by Routemaster buses some six months earlier, on 25 April 1961, and RM650, working the new 269 service, now has trolleybus No 1262 in its sights. The 641 succumbed to the inevitable on 7 November 1961, as did route 621, both photographs being taken shortly before that date. No 1262 is seen in Green Lanes, Winchmore Hill, and No 1529 in Charterhouse Street, Holborn Circus. *Marcus Eavis*

No contest

Left: Brand-new RML2319 should not have needed such a head start to pull away from this assortment of traffic in this October 1965 view in Reigate. It is interesting that the bus timetables and green LT roundel have been fixed to the old Town Hall and not to the bus shelter. *Roy Hobbs*

Common Touch

Above: The long 630 route from West Croydon to Harlesden travelled through many built-up areas, like Hammersmith and Shepherd's Bush, but the stretch across Mitcham Common was in complete contrast. No 1119 was photographed shortly before the route was withdrawn on 19 July 1960. Traffic lights now control the Beddington Lane junction, and trees and bushes obscure the open vista. *Marcus Eavis*

In Good Shape

Left: October 1969 finds Camberwell garage's RT1091 looking superb as it sits in traffic outside the National Gallery and prepares to go from a Square to an Oval! *Mike Harries*

Short Circuit

Right: This 1958 view of Class J1 No 920, built in 1938, was taken on the 'Holborn Loop'. Routes 521 and 621 ran between North Finchley and Holborn Circus, with the route numbering being determined by whether Grays Inn Road was reached before or after Farringdon Road. Route 621 trolleybuses negotiated the loop in a clockwise direction, evidenced here by the fact that No 920 is travelling southwards past Farringdon station. *Marcus Eavis*

New Coachwork

Above: Following the demotion of the last Green Line-liveried RTs to normal bus duties in 1969, advertisements were quickly applied and the gold mid-deck roundel and Green Line fleetnames removed; the influx of new Routemaster coaches, combined with service cuts, rendered the RTs superfluous. Working a bus service but still retaining its special livery is RT2252, heading down the busy A41 at Berkhamsted. *Dave Brown*

Lost in France

Right: This view of RTL1023 in August 1968 was taken nowhere near Richmond but somewhere in the South of France, on the way to Spain. In addition to providing vehicles for Continental holidays and tours, Pioneer Coaches operated route 235, which it took over from Isleworth Coaches. LT had abandoned the route in 1966 following the overtime ban earlier in the year. *Author*

Midget Submarine

Above: For most of the 1950s and '60s LT's smallest buses were the GS (Guy Special) class of 26-seaters. GS28 of Grays garage is all set to go beneath the River Thames on its journey from Kent to Essex via the Dartford Tunnel. The cost of the tolls was one of the reasons for this route lasting only two years. Of particular note in this June 1965 view at Dartford (Market Street) is the 1930s tubular bus shelter and the redundant trolleybus pole with attached street lamp. These items have now vanished, and today buses park on the opposite side of the road. Fortunately, the splendid library/museum building remains. *John Bishop*

Passing Place

Right: Class K1 No 1105 waits on the stand at Stamford Hill while Class K2 No 1207 overtakes on its way from Wood Green. The parallel wires at this point enabled the terminating 647s to be passed without the need to unhook the trolley arms. *Marcus Eavis*

Evening Extra

Above: Although route 413 was normally single-decker-operated on account of the country lanes around Brasted and Ide Hill, RTs could be found on short journeys around the busier parts. This late-summer 1969 view depicts RT3530 at Sevenoaks, travelling up from the railway station. *Dave Brown*

Fare Dealing

Right: For their first few years of service the XA-class Atlanteans were crewed, and in this view of XA12, leaving Tottenham garage in 1967, the conductor has a rare opportunity to adopt a sedentary pose. However, by the end of 1969, a start had been made on fitting fare boxes, making the XAs London's first one-person-operated double-deckers. *Marcus Eavis*

Belle of Bow

Left: Class N1 No 1610, photographed at Whipps Cross in the spring of 1959, illustrates why its home depot of Bow gained plaudits for always turning out smart vehicles. Trolleybus route 661 was withdrawn from 19 August 1959 with the introduction of replacement bus services. *Marcus Eavis*

Premature Ageing

Below left: Although Clay Hall's RTL1591 had only just entered service when photographed in March 1958, the references to 'old' are not inappropriate. Completed in 1954, the vehicle was stored along with other RTLs and RTs for four years as a result of a contraction in services. RTL1591 was only a few months at Clay Hall when this garage was closed in November 1959 following the conversion of Bow trolleybus depot to take its allocation of buses. This photograph shows Northumberland Avenue at its junction with Embankment Place. Above, Hungerford Bridge partly conceals a train standing at Platform 6 of Charing Cross station. *Marcus Eavis*

Digging for Victory

Right: For many years the height of the railway bridge at Worcester Park station was a source of irritation for LT because it precluded the use of standard-height double-deckers. Since there was no prospect of raising the railway line, a solution was found in 1963 for gaining the necessary 12in by excavating the road under the bridge (located behind the photographer). Here is RF480 in the summer of 1957. *Marcus Eavis*

Gateway to the World

Left: Before the arrival of the M4, the Heathrow Express and the Piccadilly Line extension, access to London Airport (as it was known then) from Central London was normally by airline coach down the Great West Road or by tube to Hounslow West and thence by bus. International flights at this time used the Northside terminal on the Bath Road, and T747, seen here outside Hounslow West station in 1958, could have taken you there on its way to West Drayton and Uxbridge. *Marcus Eavis*

Over the Bridge and Far Away

Above: Two 'L3'-class trolleybuses cross Kingston Bridge in 1962, shortly before the demise of the London trolleybus network after 31 years of operation. It was ironic that the first trolleybus routes were also the last. *Marcus Eavis*

Index of Locations